This book belongs to

Bookosmia

Published in 2024 by Bookosmia - India's No.1 publisher 'For kids, By kids'.
www.bookosmia.com

ISBN : 978-93-6045-113-4
Author : Siddharth Varadaprasad | Illustrator : Pooja Saklani

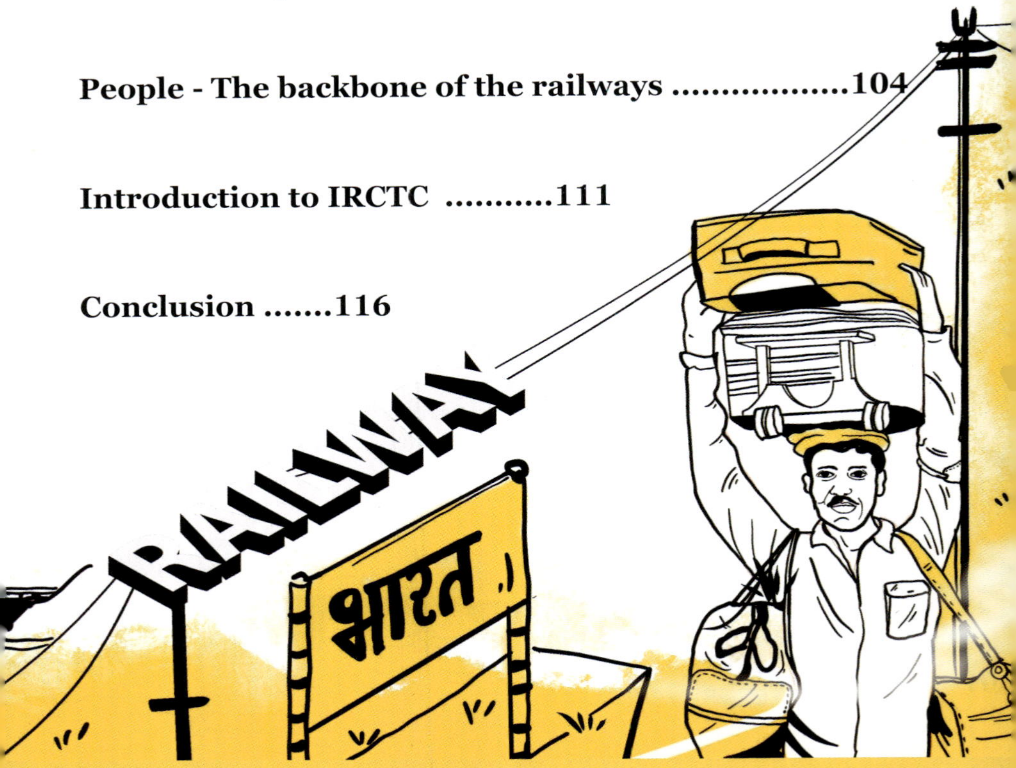
RAILWAY
भारत

FOREWORD

Indian Railways (IR), often likened to the circulatory system of the human body that moves life-giving blood to various parts of the body, is a massive enterprise that keeps the nation connected. Therefore, it is known as the lifeline of the nation.

For over 150 years, trains have inspired a blend of fear and admiration with their immense power and scale, whether as old steam locomotives or modern diesel and electric engines. Hauling extensive passenger and freight trains, Indian Railways showcases unmatched might and capability.

Initially established by the British to strengthen their empire through efficient communication and seamless governance and control, the railways also united people from different backgrounds, playing a key role during India's freedom struggle.

The nostalgic image of our Father of the Nation disembarking from a train is etched forever in the minds and conscience of the average Indian. What began with the detestable aim of subjugation transcended into interaction, unification, liberty, and eventual growth—a rich saga of legacy and romance. For much of the 20th century, rail travel was the primary mode of transport for most Indians, offering long, comfortable journeys across the country. However, the rise of affordable air travel and improved roadways in the 21st century has challenged the railways' dominance. With passengers favoring air travel for faster trips and an increase in personal car ownership and luxury bus services, the railways face a dwindling customer base.

Despite these challenges, Indian Railways is undergoing a transformation. Initiatives like the Vande Bharat semi-high-speed trains, modernized stations, new lines including connectivity to J&K with the rest of the country, high-speed rail between Mumbai and Ahmedabad, and dedicated freight corridors aim to restore its former glory.

As I often say, one can love it or hate it, but it is inconceivable to ignore IR.

The young author's book explores the intricacies of Indian Railways, offering insights into its operations and encouraging a new generation to experience the unique joys of train travel.

The book traverses the entire spectrum in an easy-to-read and illuminating manner. From explaining the technical aspects that make this mammoth enterprise function to detailing the travel options and commercials, the book helps demystify IR. It is a must-read for young adults, millennials who may not currently associate with IR but may be encouraged by the book to choose train travel for their next journey and experience the unique joys it offers.

Sudhanshu Mani
Father of Vande Bharat Trains

Sudhanshu Mani served in various senior positions in the Indian Railways for 38 years, including a stint as Railway Advisor in the Embassy of India, Berlin. He led the Train 18/Vande Bharat project, the first ever indigenous semi high-speed train of India, from concept to delivery. His journey in leading and completing this unique project is recounted in his best-seller book, 'My Train 18 Story'. He has authored six more books, including four on a subject of his special passion, art and railways, and one each on greening of environment and collation of the works of Ghālib and Shakespeare and two more books are works in progress. After retirement, he is engaged in advisory role in the corporate world, including technical, strategic and investment consulting.

FOREWORD

Siddharth's book 'Namaste Yatri' brings out his infectious and inspiring passion for trains. And why not? Trains the world over, are passionately loved by a special breed - the train lovers and Siddharth is one of them.

Indian Railways is easily the finest symbol of dynamic delivery in the nation and Siddharth's book is a laudable attempt to unfold and bring it closer to our hearts.

Ashwani Lohani

Former Chairman of the Indian Railway Board

Dr. Ashwani Lohani, IRSME 1980 (Retired) is presently working as CEO, GMRSB. Previously, he worked as the CMD of Air India on two occasions during which he helped the organization earn operating profits for two years. He also worked as the Chairman Railway Board when the railways went through major reforms resulting in impetus to the Vande Bharat train, dedicated freight corridors, high speed railway between Ahmedabad and Mumbai, cleanliness levels, improvements to infrastructure and above all a vastly improved safety record. He is the author of books like Smoking Beauties : Steam Engines of the World and Heart Over Mind.

INTRODUCTION

As children, everyone loves trains, their chugging, whistling and their clickety clack. Only a few are passionate enough to dig deep and learn about them, their rhythmic working and evolution. And then there are those rare who are so fascinated that they take up studies and further wanting to share their knowledge with the world to keep their passion going. 15-year-old Siddharth Varadaprasad is one of them.

His passion for trains and railways has made him one of the country's youngest writers on Indian Railways. His book '**Namaste Yatri : A Journey Through The Fascinating World Of Indian Railways**' delves into the history, geography and the workings of trains and railways in India, the story of how they move millions, transport freight and unite a nation. The book also narrates the life and times of people who keep the system going- day and night, 24x7. Siddharth's short and crisp explainers on railways and all-things trains in the sub-continent help give a perspective to any one who wishes to delve deeper into the subject.

Peppered with anecdotes, quizzes, trivia, fun and facts, photographs and illustrations, Siddharth's book is a kind of a dummies guide to trains and railways in India. The book does not just help one to take a train journey by offering tips on where to book a ticket and what are the various classes, but also involves pain-staking research and authenticated data on railway history, lingo and technical working. Any kid taking a train journey with elders in tow after reading this book will have an easy connect. Like the legendary Wilbert Awdry's stories of Thomas and Friends, may this book of Siddharth and trains get all the success. Chug Chug!

Rajendra B Aklekar
India's leading journalist
on Indian Railways

Deputy City Editor, Mid Day, journalist with 27+ years experience, he is the author of best-selling books on India's railway history, heritage and trains and the biographer of India's legendary railway engineer Dr E Sreedharan.

PREFACE

India. It is a beautiful country. It has so many likable things - being cosmopolitan, tasty food, diverse religions, famous monuments, having a gripping history and so much more. It also has a population of 144 crores and counting. That is a serious population for a country!

Have you ever wondered how so many people travel across India? Be it for work or travel to one's hometown or just exploring the great country. Yes, there is a transport system that allows this. Some people say that the aeroplane is the greatest invention, others say that it is the printing press. But think about this invention that allows 144 crore people to travel across India every day. I am talking about the Indian Railways! So how did the Indian Railways journey begin? What are the famous trains of India? How to book a ticket? And why is it arguably the greatest invention ever? This book is an effort to answer all these questions and more. Let's get started!

HISTORY OF INDIAN RAILWAYS

All superheroes have a challenging back story. The hero of our story, the Indian Railways, also has one.

Close your eyes and transport yourself to the 1800s. A time of great strife as the British Government began to take complete control of India, its resources and people. Governing and transportation was quite a task considering the vast country which is why Lord Dalhousie, the Governor-General of India convinced his high command to introduce a rail network in India.

Lord Dalhousie

For his vision, Lord Dalhousie is known as the father of Indian Railways till date. And so, on the sixteenth of April, 1853, the Indian Railway system was founded. The first train ran between Bori Bunder station and Thane station in Mumbai. It was operated by three steam engines reportedly called Sahib, Sindh and Sultan and ran for a distance of about 34 kilometers.

Recalling this historic event, a story in The Times of India in 2013, dug into its archives to reproduce the report that was written on that day.

News

"Nothing could've been more magnificent than the train of 20 enormous carriages with their three stupendous engines, all spick and span new, with the most perfect forms engineering could suggest, and the most beautiful tints taste could impart, occupying a line from first to last on close to four hundred feet."

By several accounts, it was a magnificent spectacle with thousands thronging to get a glimpse of this magical vehicle that could carry passengers. One can only imagine how incredible that scene would have been!

Interestingly, the railway system in India did not start with passenger service. The railways were first used to transport a variety of goods such as military artillery, construction equipment as well as important people of the British Raj. After this, a majority of trains were run to supply army utilities from one place to another. After India's freedom in 1947, Indian Railways started making rapid changes and improvements to its operations. They started phasing out steam locomotives and ran diesel locomotives instead.

Steam engine at BM Birla Planetarium in Chennai

Photo credit : The author

Steam locomotives were the past pride of Indian Railways. Indeed, they were an imposing sight as they stood as tall as the station itself on the track, ready to pull their train. Standing alongside it, a human would barely be able to reach the height of the engine wheel!

The era of steam engines ended in the nineties with the last run of Jalandhar-Firozpur Express pulled by a steam engine.

Following which, the primary source of power was diesel with trains being chugged along by the ALCO (short for American Locomotive Company) locomotives since the 1950s.

Electrification of rail routes however took place at a rapid rate and we find today a shocking shortage of the much loved 'Alcos' which would chug off into the foggy distance, having no frills but more than up for the job.

The rails also have a story in themselves. To keep up with the demand for train travel as well as the newest technology found at a global level, the railways introduced bigger rails on which wider coaches would fit. The railways took it upon themselves to change from the age-old meter and narrow-gauge lines to the newer broad-gauge tracks. Nowadays, the length of meter gauge railways is so limited that the few of them that remain have become heritage railways sites for people wanting to experience the past in the present.

Nilgiri Mountain Railway!

Photo credit : The author

From using better technologies to expanding rail routes, we see Indian Railways as it is today - the fourth largest railway network in the world with rail routes spanning from Rajasthan to Arunachal Pradesh and from Kashmir to Kanyakumari covering a route length of about sixty-five thousand kilometers!

Presently, there are a few railway lines passing through hills that have been spared from the broad-gauge conversion spree.

They offer a quaint ride up the mountains along with breathtaking views, all coupled with the customary garam chai and sometimes even ravenous monkeys who will not stop to think before climbing onto the window and grabbing any eatables they see.

The **Kalka–Shimla Railway (KSR)**, also known as the 'Toy Train', travels through the mountains and villages and passes through more than 100 tunnels. It is one of the most scenic train journeys you will ever take.

In 2008, UNESCO declared the toy train to be a World Heritage Site. A must visit for train, nature and photography lovers.

The **Darjeeling Himalayan Railway (DHR)** is a narrow-gauge railway, that is so famous that KLM Royal Dutch Airlines named one of their Boeing 777-200 ER aircrafts after it. It begins at New Jalpaiguri and terminates at Darjeeling, covering a distance of over 80 kilometers, and reaching altitudes of nearly 7500 feet.

The **Mettupalayam Ooty Railway (MMR)**, is a meter gauge line, as compared to the narrow gauge railway lines discussed earlier. It is also the only line to use the rack and pinion system in India. It utilizes this system between Coonoor and Mettupalayam to climb steep gradients present in the section.

The difference between meter gauge and narrow gauge is the **width of the track**. Narrow gauge tracks have a width of 762mm compared to meter gauge that has a width of 1000mm. Broad gauge tracks have a width of 1676mm.

The **Neral Matheran Railway**, is a narrow-gauge rail route that connects the popular hill station to Neral which is serviced by the Mumbai suburban section. It was originally financed privately, and completed in the early 20th century.

Neral Matheran loco showpiece

Neral Matheran Railway coach

Photo credit : The author

Other railway lines such as the **Pathankot-Joginder Nagar Railway** also exist and serve mainly as tourist attractions.

An important point to note is that most trains running on these routes have pairing trains that connect the origin to other metropolitan cities. For example, the Nilgiri Express connects Chennai with Mettupalayam and the train running to the hill station Ooty from Mettupalayam departs only after Nilgiri Express has arrived. This is an elegant system which ensures good connectivity for tourists from major cities.

DID YOU KNOW?

In 1853, when locals saw the first ever passenger train spewing steam and chugging along Bori Bunder and Thane, they were scared and called the train a '*Lokhandi Rakshas*' ('iron demon' in Marathi). This is documented in the book 'Halt Station India' written by Rajendra B Aklekar.

HOW RAILWAYS HAVE CHANGED

The older audience of this book are sure to remember their memories travelling by trains. For those even slightly inclined towards train travel, every trip was a special one embedded in their memory for a specific reason, be it the annoying, and persistent delay, or the delicious and steaming hot *vada pav, idly vada* or bread omelette sold by enterprising vendors!

Of course, the railways have changed a lot since its introduction in the mid 1800s. From simple additions like cushioned seats to major ones like air conditioning and track widening (gauge conversions).

The biggest change, however, was the introduction of toilets! Did you know that for the first 50 years of existence, Indian trains did not have toilets!

Thankfully that was rectified in 1902, thanks to a passenger named Okhil Chandra Sen who wrote a letter to the railway authorities describing his anguish of not having access to sanitation facilities.

While the letter leaves everyone in splits due to its colourful descriptions, it is a great reminder of how important it is to speak out in order to make a change.

Do have a look at this letter!

"

Dear Sir,

I am arrive by passenger train at Ahmedpur station and my belly is too much swelling with jackfruit. I am therefore went to privy. Just I doing the nuisance the guard making whistle blow for train to go off and I am running with lota (water pot) in one hand and dhoti (clothes) in the next. When I am fall over and expose all my shockings to man and woman on platform. I am got leaved at Ahmedpur station.

This too much bad, if passengers go to make dung, the damn guard not wait train five minutes for him? I am therefore pray your honour to make big fine on that guard for public sake otherwise I am making big report to papers.

Yours faithfull servant

Okhil Chandra Sen

"

**This is a graphic representation of the text from the original letter which is on display in the Rail Museum in New Delhi.*

Hilarious, isn't it? But also so powerful! A few decades post independence, the Indian Railways began to focus on comfort and quality with initiatives like Project Uniguage launched in the year 1992 to improve the standards of travel railways offered. The project aimed at converting most major tracks to 1676mm width so that they could accommodate wider coaches improving passenger capacity, speed and comfort.

Air conditioning (AC) was another area which the railways attended to. It simply was too uncomfortable travelling in trains for more than twenty-four hours in the sweltering summer heat of India.

The year 1956 saw the first fully air-conditioned train in India, the prestigious Poorva Express ferrying passengers between Delhi and Kolkata in the comfort of AC. A real boon in the hot summers and even the rainy monsoons as the glass windows prevented water from entering the train. The railways constantly promoted AC travel by launching the third AC coach which offered the comfort of AC at just a small premium. Furthermore, trains such as the Garib Rath and Humsafar Express made air-conditioned travel widely accessible to the masses.

The Konkan Railway Project : How this mission impossible was made possible

Enroute the Konkan Railway *Photo credit : The author*

Connectivity has always been the railways' main focus and one of its biggest challenges was establishing a rail network along the Konkan coast connecting the South West of India with the rest of the country.

Why was building a Konkan rail network a challenge?

Imagine rugged mountain terrain. Now add in loose soil, flash floods, landslides and unpredictable weather conditions. To conquer the terrain, massive bridges and multiple, long tunnels would have to be made, and made they were under the leadership of E. Sreedharan.

The project consisted of over 2000 bridges and 92 tunnels which proved to be quite a challenge. As soon as a tunnel was built it would collapse and shatter miles of progress.

However, the team led by Mr. Sreedharan was determined and completed the project in a record eight years completely decimating the proposed time period of twenty five years.

The first train to set foot, or rather wheel, on the Konkan Railway delighted everyone with its masterpiece of engineering and an unparalleled, breathtaking view.

WHO IS THE 'METRO MAN OF INDIA'?

***Elattuvalapil Sreedharan* (born 12 June 1932) is an Indian engineer who changed the face of public transport in India. Under his leadership, the challenging Konkan Railway was built. He is also known as the 'Metro Man' of India for overseeing the successful development of the Delhi Metro, which remains the template for all metro train systems built in India.**

While the Konkan Railway might have been a story of the 20th century, the railways continue to build railway lines into seemingly impossible territories like the wetlands of Meghalaya and the forestlands of Arunachal Pradesh.

One of the most interesting and challenging projects undertaken by the railways is the connection between **Katra and Banihal, in Jammu and Kashmir.**

This project involved the world's highest railway bridge christened after the river Chenab and in June 2024, the first full trial run took place after completion of construction.

Indian Railways is constantly trying to improve and offer quality service to everyone, everywhere in this beautiful country.

It truly has come a long way from the introduction of toilets to building the world's largest rail bridge.

Viewing deck on a vistadome coach — *Photo credit : The author*

Anubhuti Luxury LHB Coach — *Photo credit : The author*

How tall is the world's highest railway bridge?
Let's compare it with the Eiffel Tower in Paris!

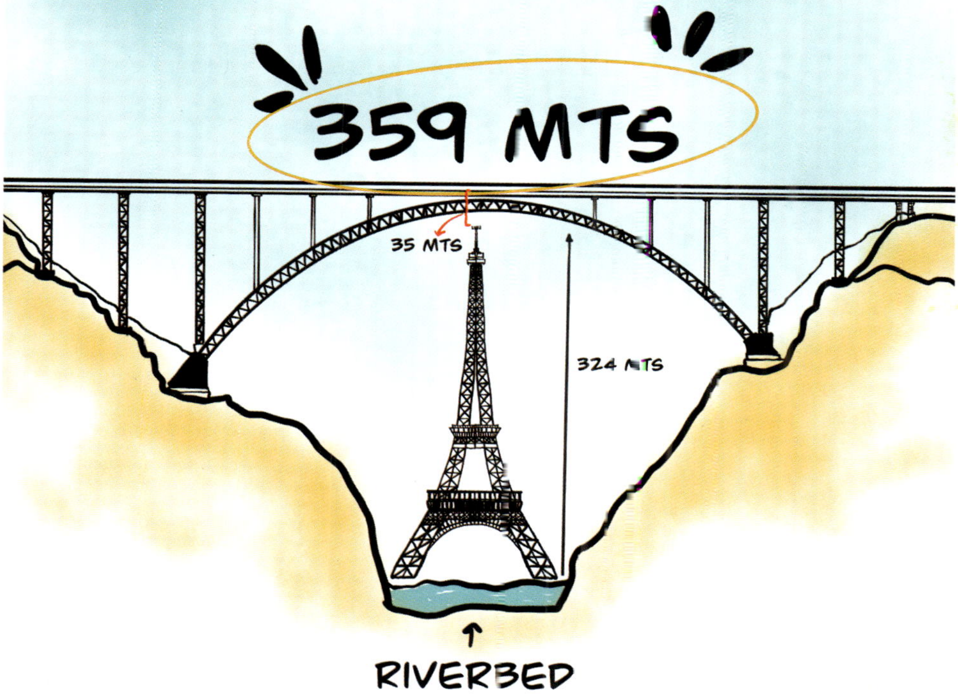

Bridge over Chenab is taller than the Eiffel Tower

UNDERSTANDING TRAIN ZONES

India is a huge country. To depict just how vast it is, a flight from Kashmir to Kanyakumari travelling at an average speed of over seven hundred kilometers per hour would still take four hours. To put it into perspective, the flight between Mumbai and Dubai takes just under four hours. To manage every rail network of India under one head would be an operational nightmare. Hence, our railway system is divided into **zones**. When the British set up railways in India, they organised it under various companies like Bombay, Baroda and Central India, Great Indian

Peninsular Railway, Southern and Mahratta Railways, East Indian Railways, etc. There were many princely states that started their own railway lines as well.

When India gained independence from British rule, the government nationalised all the railway companies into one entity called Indian Railways.

The various companies were then organised into zones under this new entity. Therefore zones like Northern Railway, Western Railway, Southern Railway and Eastern Railway came up which were nothing but the assets of the erstwhile British railway companies.

The railways excluding metros consist of eighteen zones today. Each zone is handled by a general manager who presides over the management of the zone and efficiency of the zones. Many newer railway zones have been created for administrative and operational efficiency. However, it is also argued that creation of too many railway zones leads to more bureaucratic hassles and less efficiency. What's your take?

PUT ON YOUR THINKING CAP

1. CENTRAL
2. EASTERN
3. EAST CENTRAL
4. EAST COAST
5. NORTHERN
6. NORTH CENTRAL
7. NORTH EASTERN
8. NORTHEAST FRONTIER
9. NORTH WESTERN
10. SOUTHERN
11. SOUTH CENTRAL
12. SOUTH COAST
13. SOUTH EASTERN
14. SOUTH EAST CENTRAL
15. SOUTH WESTERN
16. WESTERN
17. WEST CENTRAL
18. KONKAN

What Railway Zone do you live in? Do find out and write here

____

Photo Credit - WR Heritage -Traditions and Legend. By AK Jhingron with contributions by Rajendra B. Aklekar.

HOW DO INDIAN TRAINS WORK?

As a regular train goer, it is very easy to sometimes neglect the science behind trains and rather focus on how comfortable and fast they are. When people talk about trains they usually talk of the coaches or in Indian terms, *'Dabba'* part of the train and forget about the main part of the train that is the **engine**. Without the engine, the rest of the train would not even get a foot ahead. There are three types of railway engines : **steam, diesel and electric.**

STEAM

Steam engines were the first type of engines used to pull trains and were quite conventional in their working. The steam generated due to immense heat from the boiler (like your average tea kettle, only 10,000 times bigger!) enters a valve and creates a pressure on a piston which moves one way and then another causing the wheels of the engine to rotate. A very simple yet effective way of powering a train upto speeds of 100 kph.

Steam Engine at National Rail Museum *Photo credit : The author*

DIESEL

Diesel locomotives have an era dedicated to themselves in the vast history of Indian Railways. They pioneered rail travel with their speed and sophisticated engineering. First off, diesel locomotives are a little bit **'Team Electricity'** as well as they also use electricity partly. Diesel engines are much less complicated than electric engines. They basically just have a huge internal combustion diesel engine which are quite like the ones in our cars but much bigger. In car terms you could refer to a diesel engine in a locomotive as a V64 as they usually have 64 cylinders. The engine drives an alternator which generates alternating current (AC) and from then onwards the principle is the same as an electric locomotive.

Old Diesel Engine at National Rail Museum

Photo credit : The author

ELECTRIC

Electricity is supplied in railways from overhead cables that source it from a common grid. The electricity is then sent to a motor that is connected to the train's wheels. This motor controls the speed and power of the train. As the motor rotates, so do the wheels. Such a beautiful process – don't you agree, dear reader?

Electric engine *Photo credit : The author*

India's first electric freight locomotive class

Sir Leslie Wilson or EF/1 is India's first electric freight locomotive class introduced in 1928. Sir Leslie Orme Wilson was the Governor of Bombay in 1928 and he inaugurated the loco and hence the name. It features the original livery of India's first railway company, the Great Indian Peninsula Railway, now Central Railway. EF/1 20067 is displayed at CSMT as a heritage engine and this engine is one of the two remaining of the class, the other one being at National Rail Museum in New Delhi.

In 1942, a young boy named Christopher in England was down with measles. To cheer him up, his father Wilbert Vere Awdry made up stories about different engines in the British Railways who had personalities of their own. Seeing his son's profound enthusiasm for these stories, he sent them to a publisher and in 1945, the first book called 'The Three Railway Engines' was published. Today, we know the series distinctly thanks to the iconic blue colour steam engine with the number 1 on it. The title song goes,

"They're two, they're four,
They're six, they're eight,
Shunting trucks and
hauling freight.
Red and green and brown
and blue
They're the really useful
crew..."

CAN YOU GUESS OR FIND OUT

WHICH SERIES THIS IS?

____

ALL ABOUT RAILWAY ENGINES

By now you, dear reader, must have understood the sheer scale and magnitude of the Indian Railways. However, this would not be possible without the help of a vast workforce of dedicated engines. Each of these engines has a legacy behind them, which the new type of engines follow.

Let us now dial back in time and take a look at the majestic fleet of the steam locomotives which were kings of their era.

After India gained freedom in 1947, it was up to India to decide what type of steam locomotives it wanted to use to run its trains.

India made a fantastic choice of assembling steam engines in house and launched the wide gauge, passenger (WP) and meter gauge, passenger (YP) class of steam locomotives.

These engines were built in India as well as outside India by numerous locomotive companies, some of which were Chittaranjan Locomotive Works, TELCO, Baldwin Locomotive Works and the Canadian Locomotive Company. A total of around 750 were built and these had a glorious run for over 50 years.

The steam era came to an end on 6th December 1995 when the locomotive christened Sher-e-Punjab hauled a broad gauge train from Ferozpur to Jalandhar.

Steam engine at the National Rail Museum, Delhi

Photo credit : The author

Diesel was the next source of power for the trains of India.

Diesel locomotives were not too new, and had even been used in the steam era. The workhorse of diesel power was the Wide gauge, Diesel, Mixed traffic (WDM2) locomotive and is one of the most loved and remembered locomotives in the entire history of the railways.

WDM3A diesel engine *Photo credit : The author*

There are mainly **two types of diesel locomotives**, those built for the **meter-gauge railway** and those built for the **broad-gauge railway**. The YDM series developed from 1955 onwards (YDM1, YDM2...YDM5) represent the meter gauge diesel engines where the model names stand for meter gauge (Y), diesel(D), mixed traffic (M) and engine generation (1-5).

Along with the meter gauge diesel engines there are also a few **narrow gauge diesel engines**. As the name suggests the narrow gauge tracks were built for low capacity, inaccessible routes. The NDM and ZDM class of locomotives were built for these tracks. **Broad gauge diesel locomotives** are the ones most commonly used today and are the ones that provide for the most common type of tracks in the Indian Railways.

The WDM 2 was the most popular diesel locomotive and also the most prestigious one. This was the locomotive that would pull the all-important Rajdhani and Shatabdi trains in the diesel era when not all railway lines were electrified. The WDM 2 was followed by the WDM 3A and WDM 3D and finally the WDP4.

Unfortunately, just like how the steam era died, the diesel era is also coming dangerously close to extinction with more and more railway lines being installed with infrastructure that can support the more efficient electric traction.

WDM 3A *Photo credit : The author*

WDP 3A Toaster *Photo credit : The author*

DID YOU KNOW?

Toaster (WDP 3A), got its name because the driver cab was next to the radiator making it uncomfortably hot for the loco pilots.

The final source of power that the Indian Railways used and still uses to this day is electricity. This is the most common traction used today and has the widest variety in terms of engine types.

Fun fact : A diesel engine is actually an electric engine which is powered by a diesel motor.

WAM 4 and WAP 1 were the two electric locomotives that made electric traction popular. Next came the WAP 4, which till date is the most popular electric engine and the workhorse of the Indian Railways. This engine revolutionized electric traction and made the railways switch over from diesel to electric.

The next important electric engine to be introduced was the WAP 7. This is an extremely powerful locomotive capable of pulling 24 coaches in trains up a steep gradient without any hesitation. These superbly powerful engines are the ones that the railways is moving to today due to their reliability and power.

CAN A TRAIN HAVE MORE THAN ONE ENGINE?

Yes! In 2021, the Indian Railways created a new record with the longest-ever 2.8 kilometres freight train which pulled four trains together! This super-long train, called SheshNaag is the longest-ever train to run in the country, and was powered by four sets of electric locos! True to its name, isn't it?

WAG 1 at the National Rail Museum *Photo credit : The author*

WAG 5 hauled passenger *Photo credit : The author*

WAG 9 Freight loco *Photo credit : The author*

WAG 7 (Tigerface Bankers) at Karjat *Photo credit : The author*

Here is a list of all the broad gauge engines currently in use today, along with a few that are seen on the tracks but rarely used for passenger/goods service.

WDM 3A

WDM 3D

WDP 4

WDP 4B

WDP 4D

WDG 3A

WDM 2 – Legacy WDP 3A

(Toaster)– Legacy

WDG 4

WDG 6

WDS 6 – Shunter WAP 1

WAP 4

WAP 5

WAP 7

WAG 5

WAG 7

WAG 9

WAG 12

WAM 4 – legacy

WCAM 2 - legacy

WCAM 3

SIGNALLING SYSTEM IN RAILWAYS

I had the pleasure of speaking with Mr. N Subramanian, a retired railway official who worked in various areas primarily relating to signalling in the Western Railways for over three decades before retiring in 2006. Below is an excerpt from this discussion.

Author with Mr. N Subramanian *Photo credit : The author*

Introduction to Signalling

The word signal stands for safety. In the olden days a single line track existed between places for movement of materials and human beings and only one train could run between two stations at a time. As the requirement for movement increased, provisioning of loop lines between major train stations aided in bi-directional travel of trains. Loop lines are nothing but branching lines that move away from the main line and again join the main line after covering some distance. With this, trains could efficiently run in both directions at the same time while avoiding accidents and collisions.

Evolution of signals

The first signals were green and red flags that the station master would wave to chaperone trains. This was followed by basic signals consisting of a lamp as well as red and green tinted glass placed on an arm attached to a circle. This is called a **semaphore.**

The lamp was shone through the coloured tints and when illuminated green the driver would continue onwards and when illuminated red he would stop the train. Later, this circle based signal was divided into a lower and upper quadrant.

The lower quadrant consisted of the red and green tints however the upper quadrant consisted of green, orange and red tints. The orange was to advise the driver to slow down and proceed into the loop line.

Slowly, the lower quadrant was discarded in favour of the upper quadrant's details and signals evolved to the multi-coloured aspects we see today.

Electric signals

Over a period of time electric signals replaced manual signals and to understand this we must understand the block signalling system which is nothing but a system that divides the tracks into sections called blocks. There are 2 main types of block systems.

1. **Absolute block system** – This is used in outstation routes of lower train density and consists of a set of four signals – two before the station and two after. The signal before the station is called the home signal and the one before that is called the outer signal. The signal right at the station is called the starter signal and the one after that is called the advanced starter. In this system all signals are set to red and to allow for movement of trains they are then specifically altered to guide the driver as he moves in and out of the section. For a train to pass through a station all the four signals have to be green. By allowing only one train to remain in a block at any one point in time this system prevents accidents and collisions.

2. **Automatic block system**: Here all the signals in the block are set to green. Once a train on the main line passes a signal it then turns red to alert other trains following it that there is a train in its block and once the train has passed the section on to another one the signal turns orange. This system allows more than one train to enter between two stations.

Signalling in the railways itself is a very complex subject and a continuously evolving one as it governs the safety of the passengers and the trains.

Kavach safety system

Kavach is a Made in India ATP (automatic train protection) system that is being deployed across all routes to prevent train collisions. This system uses a set of electronic and radio frequency devices where it activates the train braking system automatically if the driver fails to control the train as per the speed restrictions. In addition, it prevents collision between two Locomotives equipped with a functional KAVACH system.

THE 'COOL KIDS' OF INDIAN RAILWAYS

All trains run on engines so they must be similar, right? Wrong! Just like each of us have different qualities and abilities, trains too are different from each other. Here are a few 'must-know' train personalities that you may have heard about often.

Train 18/Vande Bharat express *Photo credit : The author*

VANDE BHARAT EXPRESS

India had been looking for a semi high speed - bullet train for a long time and had connected with Japan numerous times for the same. However, due to political relationships as well numerous logistical issues, these projects never made it to the tracks of India. Indians never gave up and ICF (Integral Coach Factory - the production unit of Indian Railways) took it upon themselves to supply India with high speed efficient trains. These trains were welcomed joyously by most people. In the short time that Vande Bharat has existed, it has had its ups and downs with no new trains being launched for a period of 2 years partially due to the Covid pandemic and partially due to political reasons, as well as causing the unfortunate death of a few cows! Made by ICF Perambur, a rail coach factory, the Vande Bharat or Train 18 is a semi-high speed bullet-like train. As of October 2024, there are around 68 of these trains running across India.

For those interested in taking this next generation speed king of Indian Railways, some examples are Delhi-Varanasi, Delhi- Amb Andaura, Delhi-Katra, Mumbai-Ahmedabad, Nagpur-Bilaspur, Chennai-Mysuru, to mention a few.

Launched on the 15th of February 2019 to run between New Delhi and Varanasi, this train is equipped with best of class luxuries, catering and staff.

Completing the route in a time of 8 hours with an average speed of approximately 95 km/h and reaching a maximum speed of 130 km/h, it is the fastest train running on that route as well as the fastest Vande Bharat Express.

WHO IS THE FATHER OF THE VANDE BHARAT?

Sudhanshu Mani is considered the father of the Vande Bharat train set and it is his contribution that transformed a dream into a reality - the nation's dream of manufacturing a semi high-speed train set that rivalled the likes of modern trains in many developed countries.

An engineer with a career with the railways that spanned over thirty years, Mr. Mani was the clear choice amongst many who would have to undertake the mammoth task of producing a train 18 set within a timespan of just one and a half years (18 months).

He was the General Manager of Integral Coach Factory which was tasked with producing the first prototype of such a train and this prototype still runs between Varanasi and New Delhi now for over a period of 5 years and has covered many hundreds of thousands of kilometers. It was produced at a record low cost of about Rs. 100 crores, an unmatched feat.

Vande Bharat *Photo credit : The author*

RAJDHANI EXPRESS

Rajdhani Express *Photo credit : The author*

Rajdhani means 'capital' and true to its name, the Rajdhani Express trains are run only between the capital city of India, Delhi and different state capitals of India.

On March 1, 1969,the first 9 car Rajdhani Express was flagged off between New Delhi and Howrah. The train completed the 1450 Kms trip in 17 hours and 20 minutes.

Rajdhani Express Trains are fully air conditioned, super fast trains and stop only at important stations. Hence the age old saying :

"Why are you in such a hurry? Do you have to catch a Rajdhani?"

Delhi Special Rajdhani at Bandra Terminus *Photo credit : The author*

Trivandrum Rajdhani at Goa *Photo credit : The author*

These trains, like the Vande Bharat Express, offer very good service and catering. But unlike the Vande Bharat Express, they are sleeper trains and most importantly, Rajdhani trains have an edge when it comes to being luxurious and offering premium travel experience.

This class and premium service we speak of comes at a price though, I must warn you and first class fares can sometimes surpass air fares for this route. On the Mumbai Rajdhani, a third-class AC ticket will cost about 1500 rupees, second-class will cost you 2500 rupees and a first-class ticket will cost you a whopping 5000 rupees! *

**Prices as on March 2024*

TEJAS EXPRESS

Mumbai-Madgaon Tejas with Vistadome

Photo credit : The author

These trains are a high speed and luxurious variant of the Shatabdi Express. Sadly, they have been abandoned in favor of the better made Vande Bharat Express.

SHATABDI EXPRESS

The Shatabdi trains are fast, fully air-conditioned sitting trains under a route distance of 700 kilometers.

Examples of Shatabdi trains are :

- ***Chennai - Mysuru Shatabdi***
- ***Delhi- Kathgodam Shatabdi***
- ***New Delhi - Bhopal Shatabdi***. *(The longest Shatabdi with a route distance of exactly 700 kilometers)*

Mysuru-Chennai Shatabdi Express *Photo credit : The author*

Shatabdi Express was launched first in the year 1988. They, like the other types of trains we have discussed so far, have excellent catering and service.

The Gatimaan Shatabdi between New Delhi and Jhansi travels at 160 km/h making it one of the fastest trains in terms of speed in the Indian Railways (now the distinction is shared with Vande Bharat Express).

DURONTO EXPRESS

Duronto Express trains are very fast sleeper trains which travel from one place to another with very few halts. Back when they were launched, they were supposed to only have technical halts which included halts for crew change, locomotive change etc, however as demand surged, the railways decided to add stops in major passing cities for the Duronto Express.

It was first launched in 2009 by Ms. Mamata Banerjee, the then railway minister of Indian Railways. She launched a train with only technical halts between New Delhi and Sealdah (Another one of Kolkata's railway stations) and called it Duronto.

Duronto Express *Photo credit : The author*

Catering and service is very good on these trains. You will mostly find Duronto trains running on routes which are able to allow for decent speeds and which connect to metropolis cities.

PUT ON YOUR THINKING CAP

'Duronto' is a word from Bengali. What does it mean when loosely translated into English? Circle the right one from the options below :

1. **Luxurious**
2. **Uninterrupted**
3. **Powerful**

Answer : 2. Uninterrupted

ANTYODAYA EXPRESS

These trains are fast, general seating trains. This means that people can travel on these trains even without a reserved seat. There is no berth/seat allocation and any number of people that can fit in can travel in a coach.

HUMSAFAR EXPRESS

Humsafar Express can be looked upon as the successor of the Garib Raths. While they consist of the same third tier coaches present in Garib Raths, these coaches are slightly more modern and improved with a few more features here and there.

Humsafar Express *Photo credit : The author*

GARIB RATH EXPRESS

Garib Rath means a chariot for the poor in Hindi and that is exactly what Mr. Lalu Prasad Yadav, the then Rail Minister's idea was. Basically, he wanted economically-challenged people to travel in decently comfortable trains. That is what the Garib Rath offers.

It is a fully air conditioned, three tier (We will be discussing what a 'tier' means in the coming chapters) sleeper train.

An example of a Garib Rath Express would be the Dhanbad – Bhubaneswar Garib Rath Express. This train travels through the economically backward area of Jharkhand and therefore fulfills its model as being a comfortable option of travel for people living in rural areas.

This train was cancelled shortly after the Covid 19 pandemic. Another example of a Garib Rath still running is the Delhi - Chennai Garib Rath which covers the longest distance of its type.

Garib Rath Express *Photo credit : The author*

DOUBLE DECKER EXPRESS

Yes it is exactly what it sounds like! It is a great experience to travel on the top tier of a double decker train and is part of every rail fan's bucket list.

Examples of popular double-decker express trains would be Chennai-Bangalore, Mumbai-Ahmedabad and Mumbai-Goa (now discontinued). These type of trains are generally run on short, sitting, high density routes. However, due to their lack of patronage, there are very few running today in India.

Double Decker Express *Photo credit : The author*

SUPERFAST EXPRESS

Don't go by its name. Superfast Expresses aren't that fast. They just travel from place to place stopping at junctions in between at reasonable speeds.

They do not cost a lot and have mediocre service. While there are a few exceptional superfast trains like Poorva and Tamil Nadu Superfast Express that travel as fast as Garib Raths, they are very few in number.

Jaipur Superfast Express *Photo credit : The author*

PUT ON YOUR THINKING CAP

What do you think is the criteria for a train to be classified as super fast? Circle the right option.

1. **Average speed over 55 km/h**
2. **Average speed over 70 km/h**
3. **Nothing to do with speed, it's just a title**

Answer : 1. Average speed over 55 km/h

Until now we have only looked at passenger trains. We also know that there are freight trains run by the Indian Railways. But this is not all, there are other special trains which are run by Indian Railways. They are not run everyday or every week. They are run only during specific dates.

WHAT IS A SPECIAL TRAIN?

There are many trains that run from Mumbai to Nagpur - a wide variety too like Duronto Express and Superfast Express. But during special months such as Diwali there is an extra train run for the cause of workers who work in Mumbai but whose family live in Nagpur and want to visit their family during the Diwali break. Due to this extra load of passengers, an extra train under the category of Festival Specials is run.

DID YOU KNOW?

The longest train journey one can take in India is on Vivek Express from Kanyakumari in Tamil Nadu to Dibrugarh in Assam and this takes around 75 hours to complete.

THE CLASS TOPPERS

Presenting the class toppers or the 'creme de la creme' (if you feel like they deserve a fancy title) of Indian Railways. Yes, as a train, they do take passengers from one place to another but believe it or not, that's not the primary goal! There is a saying, 'The journey is better than the destination', well, that's exactly what these trains provide as they are for people who want to travel in a train and see India in style.

These trains have every luxury you would expect. From restaurants to ballrooms...what do you feel about attending a dance party aboard a train? Here are a few such uber luxurious trains.

PALACE ON WHEELS

The Palace on Wheels is a luxury train that tours Rajasthan. It starts from New Delhi and covers Jaipur, Sawai Madhopur, Jaisalmer, Jodhpur, Udaipur and Agra. Then it returns to Delhi. A ticket on the Palace on Wheels would cost you about one and half lakh rupees per day and you can book it online on the IRCTC website.

ROYAL ORIENT

The Royal Orient covers Gujarat and a bit of Rajasthan. It starts from Delhi and covers Jaipur, Udaipur, Ahmedabad, Junagarh, Veraval and Mandvi.

MAHARAJAS' EXPRESS

The Maharajas' Express covers Rajasthan and Uttar Pradesh. It starts from Delhi and covers northern India for 7 days.

FAIRY QUEEN

Fairy Queen is the world's oldest running steam locomotive and is run as a heritage train from Delhi to Alwar and back.

THE LEGACY TRAINS

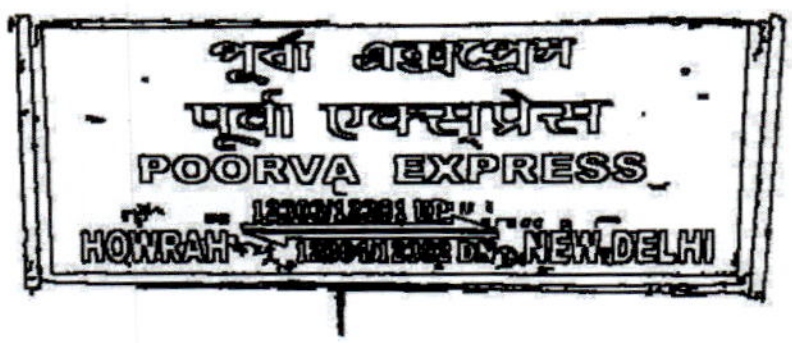

Air India's magnificent 747 named Akbar, the towering INS Vikrant, even the small yet majestic Maruti 800 are some of India's most cherished and respected machines. However, nothing is cherished more than the gentle, age-old hoot to which millions have woken up, eager to meet their near and dear ones. This chapter is about certain trains of India that have risen to the nation's calling for decades and even centuries, transporting passengers tirelessly to the remotest of regions in this magnificent country.

THE FRONTIER MAIL

This old beauty was inaugurated in the 1920s and served the busy route between Mumbai and Peshawar during a time period when there were no political divides between the two metropolitan cities. Its destination had to be shortened to Amritsar after the partition and its name re-christened to the Golden Temple Mail.

GRAND TRUNK EXPRESS

Grand Trunk Express is a daily super fast between Delhi and Tambaram, a town near Chennai. Initially when inaugurated in 1929, it originated at Peshawar and terminated at Mangalore, however subsequently it was made to depart from Delhi and terminated at Chennai. This train (usually abbreviated to GT Express) holds a special place in many Tamilian's hearts as it was the only way to get to the capital city of India from Tamil Nadu for quite a long time. However it was outdone by the fancy, shiny Tamil Nadu Express in 1976 and subsequently, the barrage of high speed trains that soon took over the route.

THE BOAT MAIL

A small fish, braving the torrential sea and ferrying passengers diligently from Madras (Chennai) to the island town of Rameswaram for over 100 years. This train is a household name for most Tamilians, providing easy access for worship in the temple town. Its history is one of a martyr's, derailing in the horrific tsunami of the 1960s and still cruising over the Pamban bridge day in and day out. It is now known as The Rameswaram Express.

Boat mail *Photo credit : The author*

POORVA EXPRESS

One of the first trains to reach the 130 kmph mark, connecting Delhi to Kolkata in less than 20 hours has made this train somewhat of an icon with Bengalis and has put it (arguably) in league with the famous Rasgulla!

DECCAN QUEEN

This was introduced as a luxury train between Mumbai and Pune in 1930 aptly named after Pune, which is also known as ''Queen of Deccan'' (Dakkhan chi Rani). Initially, the train was introduced with 2 rakes of 7 coaches each one of which was painted in silver with scarlet mouldings and the other with royal blue with gold lines.

The coaches of the original rakes were replaced in 1966 by anti-telescopic steel bodied integral coaches built by ICF, Perambur. Over a period of time the coaches underwent significant improvements to their interiors. The distinctive color scheme of cream and oxford blue with red band above the window level was adopted as the colour scheme for this train.

One of the unique features of this train is the dining car with cushioned chairs and carpets which offers table service and has modern pantry facilities. This is not just a mere transportation medium but a piece of history that people experience while travelling on it and the train has a set of loyal followers.

PUNJAB MAIL

Punjab Mail is over 16 years older than the more glamorous Frontier Mail. It is estimated that the train first ran on 1st June 1912 between Mumbai and Peshawar from Ballard Pier Mole and covered this distance in about 47 hours. Ballard Pier Mole station was actually a hub for GIPR (Great Indian Peninsular Railway) services. During the pre-partition period, the Punjab Limited as she was then called, was the fastest train in British India. Post independence this train was truncated at Firozpur.

GITANJALI EXPRESS

The first train to cross the 100 kmph barrier in India, it ran the high-density route between Mumbai and Kolkata at tremendous speed and efficiency.

RAILWAYS AND THE INDIAN FREEDOM STRUGGLE

The role of the Indian Railways during the freedom struggle is often overlooked. Interestingly, the railways evoked multiple layers of emotion. On one hand, it was seen as a symbol of colonialism by the people of India. Tired of being discriminated in their own country and forced to travel in inhumane conditions, revolutionaries mounted multiple attacks on trains - aiming to hit the British's administration's lifeline. On the other hand, the railway network managed to connect Indians like nothing else could. Freedom fighters traveled in huge groups to different places and gathered support and funds from the huge crowds that gathered to see them in railway stations, making them impromptu public rallies. Let's revisit some significant incidents involving the Indian Railways from our days of freedom struggle.

DISRUPTING RAILWAYS AS A WAY TO PROTEST

KAKORI TRAIN ROBBERY

In August 1925, Indian revolutionaries Ram Prasad Bismil and Ashfaqullah Khan of the Hindustan Republican Association (HRA) decided to rob a train at a place called Kakori near Lucknow. The train was believed to be transporting money to the British treasury (taxes paid by Indians). Looting the train had a dual purpose : first to protest against the unjust taxes on Indians and second to utilise the money for their activities at the HRA. This robbery and the manner in which it was executed sent shock waves across the British empire and they left no stone unturned to capture the revolutionaries.

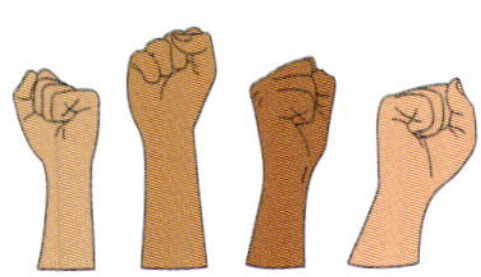

ATTACK ON ANDREW FRASER

In 1907, several attempts were made to derail the trains carrying Andrew Fraser, Lieutenant-Governor of Bengal who had been a key member in the partioning of Bengal. Later that year, a bomb was also thrown at his train but Fraser escaped.

MAHATMA GANDHI'S TOOL OF CONNECTIVITY

The railways became a symbol of Mahatma Gandhi's connection with people across the world. He always travelled in the Third Class compartment and wherever he went, hundreds of people gathered to receive him and to hear him speak. They also donated for his funds and followed him as he went on road rallies.

In 1946, Gandhi toured the country by train to raise awareness against untouchability, which was prevalent in those days.

PUT ON YOUR THINKING CAP

In 1893, Mahatma Gandhi, then a young lawyer, was on a train in South Africa. The events of that day played a crucial role in his commitment for the oppressed. What was the incident? If you do not know, ask your parents or teacher about it and write it here.

COMMON ABBREVIATIONS AND TERMS

When you are aboard a train, sometimes on long journeys, there is nothing much to do. During such times, you may end up exploring the train and reading various abbreviations on the coaches - both inside and outside the train. Here is your guide to understanding them better.

These are the abbreviations for the type of coaches. ICF stands for Integral Coach Factory (ICF) and LHB stands for Linke Hofmann Busch (LHB) coaches.

LHB coaches are newer, safer coaches that can travel at faster speeds and are rapidly replacing the ageing ICF coaches.

Atmanirbhar Bharat Coach (Self- Reliant India)

Photo credit : The author

Coaches are manufactured in three main plants. Rail Coach Factory, Kapurthala (RCF), Integral Coach Factory, Perambur (ICF) and Modern Coach Factory, RaeBareilly (MCF). Majority of the coaches seen today in the railways come from RCF and ICF.

CHAIR CAR / SLEEPER CAR

Coaches need to suit the different specifications of trains in the Indian Railways. Broadly these specifications can be satisfied by two types - chair car and sleeper. Further, these are divided into AC and non-AC.

The top sleeper berth in a First AC coach

Photo credit : The author

As the names suggest, chair car refers to coaches with seats for short travel and sleeper refers to coaches made for overnight, long distance trains.

All coaches include basic features such as lights, windows and western/Indian style restrooms however newer coaches such as those found in premium trains like the Vande Bharat and Tejas Express have additional provisions such as aircraft style vacuum toilets, automated doors, retractable tables, reclining seats and even entertainment screens on every seat.

Tejas express *Photo credit : The author*

Tiers : H A B S C D PC UR E M K EV

There is a specific naming system for coaches based on their tiers. These are listed below

H = First class sleeper.
A = Second class sleeper.
B = Third class sleeper.
S = Non-AC sleeper.
C = Air-conditioned chair cars.
D = Non-AC chair cars.
PC = Pantry car where food is prepared and stored on certain long-distance trains.
UR/GS = Unreserved/General seating.
E = Executive class chair cars.
M = Third AC Economy
K = Anubhuti Class (Executive Class)
EV = Vistadome coach on scenic routes

In most trains, there are a certain number of coaches of one type, these coaches are designated by numbers. For example, the fifth AC Three Tier coach would be named as B+5, B5.

FIRST CLASS

First class coaches are the epitome of luxury. Their lockable cabin doors and spacious legroom are quite tempting, however all this does come at a hefty price. There is usually none or one first class coach on a train. This is because of their price which at times closely matches air fares. This really brings up the question as to why anyone would travel in first class. However, true rail fans would know and appreciate the opulence and experience first class offers!

SECOND AC

Second AC is the next best option in terms of comfort and convenience. The prices often undercut airfares which makes it a sensible travel option especially for short distances.

THIRD AC

Third AC is the most economical way of travelling in comfort. Lets face it, no one likes travelling for 24 hours in the sweltering summers of India and Third AC provides for a comfortable medium of travel that will not blow too big a hole in your pocket.

UNRESERVED COACHES

Unreserved coaches are coaches available for travel without prior reservation. In short, there are no seat allocations and the number of people can be higher than the number of seats.

FREIGHT TRAINS

When one mentions the Indian Railways, the first thought is about the passenger operations, but freight operation is also an interesting and important topic to speak about. Freight trains play a key role in the Indian economy by transporting vital goods across the country.

This includes coal and oil that are extremely important in providing electricity, and power.

Other important substances such as minerals like bauxite and iron ore which are needed for important processes, are also transported by the railways.

Container Train *Photo credit : The author*

Freight trains are a cheap way of transporting voluminous goods across India and are hence favoured over the more expensive air cargo.

In fact, freight trains are so popular that they can even stretch up to three and a half kilometers. Another use of freight trains is to transport newly manufactured vehicles across India from their manufacturing headquarters.

They also provide assistance to truck drivers by allowing the trucks to be loaded onto the train and be transported along routes where the road connectivity is not that good. This is an efficient system for the truck drivers as it saves them diesel as well as their energy.

Just like in passenger trains, goods trains also have specific coaches designed to carry various types of goods. Here are the coaches one may expect to find as part of a goods train.

Open wagon.
Covered wagon.
Box wagon.
Tank wagon.
Well wagon.
Flat wagon.
Hopper wagon.

Unfortunately, freight trains are one of the slowest types of trains in the Indian Railways and have an average speed of twenty to thirty km/h. This is why the railways are developing dedicated freight corridors in the hope of speeding up freight trains.

Goods Wagon

Photo credit : The author

There are currently two dedicated freight corridors - the Eastern Dedicated Freight Corridor (EDFC) between Firozpur and Dankuni, West Bengal which was completed late 2023.

The Western Dedictated Freight Corridor (WDFC) between Dadri on the outskirts of Delhi and Jawaharlal Nehru Port Trust (JNPT) in Mumbai is ready upto the outskirts of Mumbai (New Palghar) and should reach JNPT within a year.

PUT ON YOUR THINKING CAP

If you were in-charge of deciding the lunch menu for passengers on a long-distance train, what are the items you would choose?

HOW DO I? A PRACTICAL GUIDE FOR NEW TRAVELLERS.

If you have never booked a train ticket or need help guiding you on your first train journey, this is the place to be. Here are some practical questions answered to help you enjoy your travel without being bogged down by challenges.

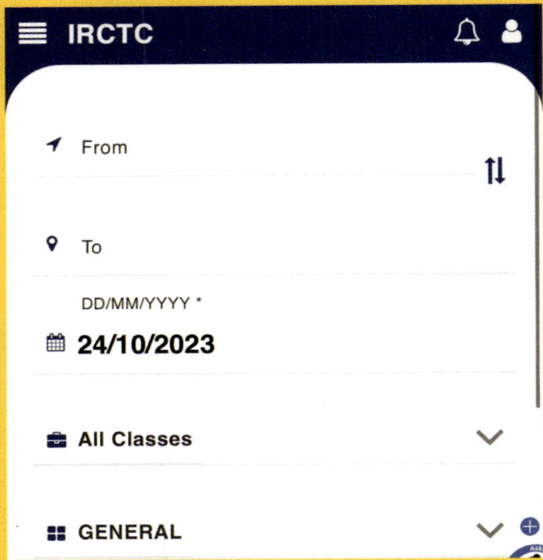

1. Log on to the IRCTC website - https://www.irctc.co.in.

2. Insert origin and destination into the system, as well as date of travel.

3. Select any one train from the list that the website provides.

4. Proceed to pay.

A very simple and efficient process compared to the long lines one would see at the ticket counters in the days before the internet!

PRO TIPS FOR YOUR TRAIN JOURNEY

- Book your ticket at least a month in advance for high density routes to make sure that good seats are available. It is also best to select berth and meal preferences ahead of time.

- Arrive on the platform in good time before the train's arrival. My aunt once was running late for her Rajdhani Express from Mumbai Central and tried to call the station manager to see if the train could be delayed a little bit!

- If you are travelling on a train which does not serve complimentary food, it is always best to get ample food from home. While food might be available to purchase, everyone agrees that there is nothing better than clean, home-cooked food!

- While on the train, **DO NOT LEAN OUTSIDE THE DOOR.** This is extremely unsafe especially when there are sudden abrupt movements of the coach and poles and other items may hit you and knock you out.

- Do not forget to bring earplugs and an eye-mask. You never know if the person next to you might snore!

Photo credit : The author

- Try to look out of the window at all times. Trains are a medium of transport that really allow one to experience the exhilarating beauty of India in all its glory. Just waking up to the sight of lush green fields is a sight to behold.

- Be relaxed. Trains are built to withstand all kinds of weather. In case of lightning one must always remember that a coach is an example of Faraday's cage which prevents voltage from being conducted.

- Do not get in or out of a running train.

- **Absolutely do not take selfies near railway tracks. This practice is sadly followed to this day even after numerous deaths.**

- Be generous. In premium trains, servers might ask for tips in which case it is always best to oblige as in most cases they work extremely hard to please the customer in return for very less pay.

- Lastly, don't forget to enjoy the experience!

Photo credit : The author

PUT ON YOUR THINKING CAP

Railways have been the setting for many blockbuster films and songs. Think of Shahrukh Khan and Malaika Arora dancing 'Chaiya Chaiya' on the top of a moving train or the heart wrenching climax scene of 'Sadma' starring Kamal Haasan and Sridevi. Which other movie or song shot on trains can you recall?

PEOPLE - THE BACKBONE OF THE RAILWAYS

Indian Railways is not just all about locomotives and coaches. Just like a company without its employees is nothing, the railways is nothing without numerous individuals such as conductors, engineers, pointsmen etc.

Toaster with crew *Photo credit : The author*

Refuelling of a generator car in progress *Photo credit : The author*

Everyday, thousands of maintenance staff ensure that the tracks spanning the entirety of the railways are kept in shape and are safe to protect the lives of the millions travelling by trains every single day. They make sure that the tracks have not expanded too much are not obstructed in anyway.

Motorman *Photo credit : The author*

Pointsmen ensure that the points deciding the course of the train are appropriate and prevent collisions. They take part in an important procedure known as the **route relay interlocking system.**

This is where the pointsmen set the points towards a particular direction and lock the points using a key. This ensures that the particular section of track is locked on a specific course.

This key is then delivered to the train driver who passes the key to the pointsman present at the next station who proceeds to unlock the section.

The interlocking system is integrated with the signal. Once the route is set and the tracks are aligned in a particular direction, the same is conveyed to the engine driver through a system of signals.

The interlocking between the railway track and the signal in the system is what gives it the name of route relay interlocking system. These days, a very complex and sophisticated computer based electronic interlocking system is the mainstay of Indian Railways.

Central Railway control room *Photo credit : The author*

Other jobs in the railways relate to customer satisfaction for e.g. railway caterers who prepare sumptuous food served hot and ticket collectors who check that everyone on board has a valid ticket.

There is a slogan that says, **"Once a railway person, always a railway person."** This statement is brought to life by the numerous railway workers who have worked their entire lives serving the nation.

Many veterans such as M. Kalavathy, the first woman signal engineer and E. Sreedharan, popularly known as the 'Metro Man of India' due to his visionary work, have dedicated their services to the railways and will be etched in railway history for years to come.

DID YOU KNOW?

New Delhi's National Rail Museum is the first railway museum set up in India

Photo credit : The author

Bholu the elephant is the Indian Railways mascot

COOL FACTS

Chenab rail bridge in Jammu and Kashmir at a height of around 360m is the world's tallest railway bridge.

The station with the shortest name in India is 'Ib' in Odisha and the station with the longest name is 'Puratchi Thalaivar Dr. M.G. Ramachandran Central Railway Station' (known as Chennai Central to most of us).

Nagpur in Maharashtra has a diamond crossing where trains can run in all four directions.

SSS Hubballi in Karnataka has the longest platform in the world with a length of 1507 m.

INTRODUCTION TO IRCTC

IRCTC

IRCTC provides ticketing, catering and tourism services to the Indian Railways. It is a publicly listed company with the Government of India being the major shareholder. Prior to the introduction of IRCTC, one would have to visit their nearest station and purchase tickets from the ticketing office. This proved to be a cumbersome process and often resulted in mile long queues that people would have to stand in only to figure out that the train was full.

IRCTC has tackled all of these problems with their online website which takes city pairs as well as dates of travel as input and outputs all the trains running between the two places on the selected day, along with the availability of seats in different classes with prices. IRCTC also runs special trains for tourism purposes, examples of which would be the Bharat Gaurav Express and the Ramayan Express. Nowadays IRCTC also allows plane and hotel bookings via their website and allows the user to plan a comfortable trip all from one portal.

Saloon Car *Photo credit : The author*

Hiring a coach :

There is a niche service provided by the Indian Railways where you can rent the general manager's coach all for yourself. This stellar coach consists of a living room, several bedrooms, a kitchen, a viewing deck, as well as an attendant who will accompany you throughout your travels, and this coach can accommodate ten to twelve individuals comfortably. Essentially a house on wheels, this coach is used by some of the senior most railways personnel including the Railway Minister himself, and is truly a one off experience that every rail fan must indulge in to satisfy the itch for travelling in the shoes of an important official. Please do try it out!

DID YOU KNOW?

Train food

Photo credit : The author

You can now order food online through your smartphone while inside a train from food outlets at various stations enroute.

Now that you have read this book, let's see how much you remember.

Who is known as the 'Metro Man of India'?

Answer :

Which train also means uninterrupted in Bengali?

Answer :

What is the name of the Indian railway's mascot?

Answer :

What is the name of the website where you can book tickets online?

Answer :

The railway station with the shortest name in India is?

Answer :

Answers : 1.E. Sreedharan 2. Duronto Express 3. Bholu 4. Irctc.co.in 5. Ib in Odisha

WHAT'S YOUR TRAIN STORY? WRITE OR DRAW ABOUT YOUR TRAIN JOURNEY EXPERIENCE BELOW...

....

....

....

....

....

....

....

....

....

....

....

....

....

....

....

....

Great work! Now take a picture of this page, send it to sara@bookosmia.com and get published on Bookosmia, India's No. 1 publishing destination for kids!

CONCLUSION

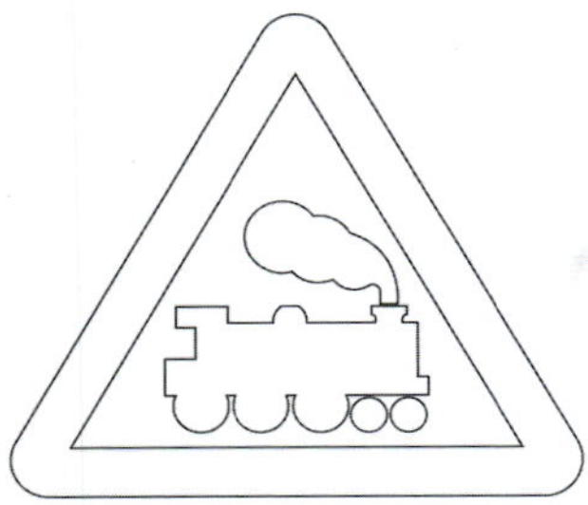

Dear reader, kindly take out two minutes to read this page. I hope this book has been as good a journey for you as it has been for me. There are many people in India who look down upon trains and consider them inferior, and it would be my utmost pleasure if this book has convinced some of them to think again. The purpose of writing this book was to help educate a variety of people on the subject, from ten year olds to senior citizens.

If you gained even a speck of wisdom that was to your liking from reading this book, then my goal has been accomplished. I like to think of this analogy which sums up my experience writing this book.

I started off in the wilderness on the banks of the Vaitarna river, charging purposefully uphill towards the quaint station of Vaitarna. Once I reached there, I stood transfixed, thinking of how I would proceed forward. Out of thin air, a 12 coach local train heading towards Churchgate stormed into the station and suddenly, I knew what path lay in front of me, and what I had to do next.

Vaitarna *Photo credit : The author*

Vaitarna station *Photo credit : The author*

I hopped onto the train as it left Vaitarna. Five minutes passed and the train stopped at the next station Virar. In this pattern, the local train chugged along as it passed many more stations towards its end goal, Churchgate. I realized that the train was my guide through this journey, always pulling me along the right track and before I knew it, the train and I had reached Churchgate.

So here we are, dear reader, the train and me, at the end of the track, waving to you one final goodbye as we part ways into the deep mist.

Sunset by the tracks

Pamban bridge

Information board at Karaikkudi Station

Certificate of meritorious service awarded by Indian Railways in 1972

Western Railway headquarters

ACKNOWLEDGEMENTS

I owe a debt of gratitude to my publisher Bookosmia and my mentor Ms. Archana Mohan for guiding and motivating me throughout the process, as well as standing by me from start to finish.

I thank Mr. Rajendra B. Aklekar for reviewing the draft and providing his myriad ideas and his enthusiasm that shaped the final version. It was an honour to meet another railway fan a thousand times more passionate about the subject. Meeting him was a big fan moment for me as he is the author of some of the best selling books on the history and heritage of Indian Railways and also the biographer of the well-known legend Mr. Sreedharan. He is very popular among the rail enthusiasts and has been instrumental in setting up the Rail Heritage Gallery at the CSMT station. What struck me at my first meeting with him was how humble and grounded he is as a person despite so many accolades and how his passion for the subject shines through every time as he continues to encourage and motivate me in my journey as a writer.

I would like to thank my father for nurturing the love of trains in me from the time I was a toddler and for spending countless hours on all those train journeys with me - equally fascinated and wide eyed by all the beauty around.

I would like to thank my mother for indulging my father and me with all those train journeys and accompanying us on most and for encouraging me to write this book and finding a way to make it happen.

Finally, I would like to thank my grandparents , my uncles and aunts for all their love through this book writing process without ever finding fault with anything and being ever ready to find time for me to support and encourage.

Lastly, thank you readers for reading my maiden book. Hope you enjoyed reading it as much as I did writing it.

ABOUT THE AUTHOR

Meet Siddharth Varadaprasad, a talented fifteen - year-old budding writer hailing from Mumbai, India. For the past four years, he has been crafting captivating articles and enchanting short stories.

Siddharth's model train set

Mr. Rajendra B. Aklekar and Siddharth

Acrylic painting gifted to the author by artist Vidya Ramanathan, the author's maternal grandmother.

When not lost in the world of words, you can find him transported to tracking railroads and engines. Siddharth's fascination with the Indian Railways began at the tender age of seven, and over time, he has become an expert on the subject. After over a year of dedicated effort and research and interaction with stalwarts in the field, he has condensed his vast knowledge into this very book. An active contributor to Bookosmia (India's No.1 Publisher 'for kids, by kids across 150+ locations), Siddharth thoroughly enjoys writing for them and engaging in interviews.

BIBLIOGRAPHY

Websites:

www.indiarailinfo.com
www.indianrailways.gov.in
www.irctc.co.in
www.irfca.org
www.erail.in
www.railenthusiastindia.org.in
www.railmitra.com

Books:

- Halt Station India - Dr. Rajendra B. Aklekar
- A Short History of Indian Railways - Dr. Rajendra B. Aklekar
- Indian Railways: A visual journey - DK series